Wedding March

from "A Midsummer Night's Dream"
by Felix Mendelssohn

arranged for harp by Sylvia Woods

Felix Mendelssohn composed the "Wedding March" in 1842 as a part of his suite for Shakespeare's play <u>A Midsummer Night's Dream</u>. It is most commonly played as a wedding recessional.

This sheet music includes two harp arrangements. The first is for intermediate to advanced lever harp players, or pedal harpists.

The second arrangement is a bit easier. It can be played on small harps with 22 or more strings, from C to C.

Wedding March
from A MIDSUMMER NIGHT'S DREAM
Intermediate to advanced harp arrangement

Lever harp players: before you begin, set the high D# and F# levers as shown above.
Sharping lever changes are indicated with diamond notes and also with octave wording. Pedal changes are written below the bass staff.

When there are split stems, the downstem notes are played with the left hand.
The D notes in parentheses may be omitted on lever harps to facilitate the lever changes.

by Felix Mendelssohn
harp arrangement by Sylvia Woods

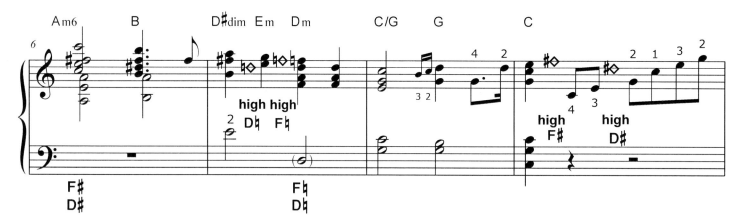

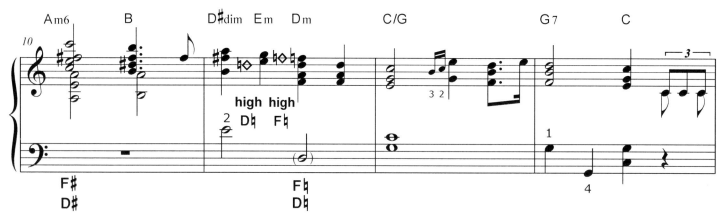

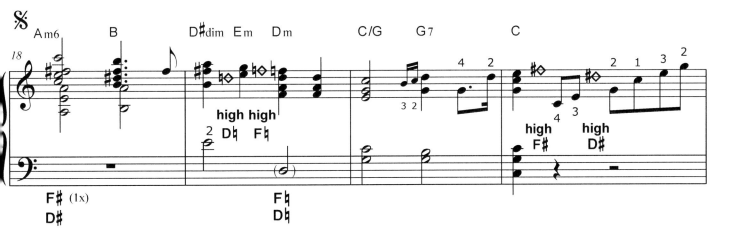

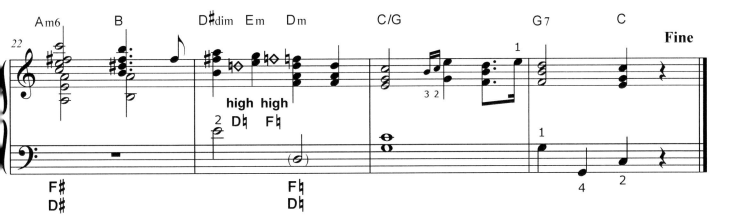

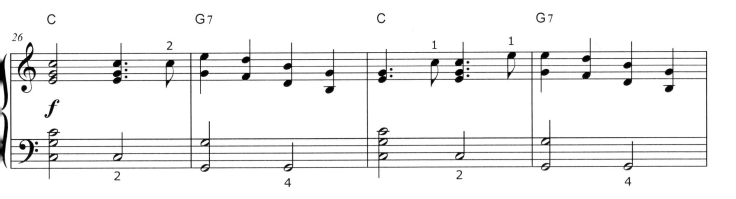

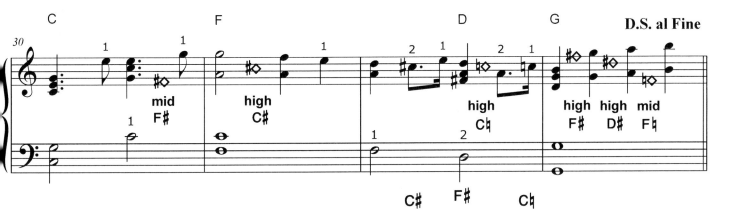

Wedding March

from A MIDSUMMER NIGHT'S DREAM

Easier harp arrangement, playable on small harps

Before you begin, set the D# and F# levers as shown above.
Sharping lever changes are indicated with diamond notes and also with octave wording.
When there are split stems, the downstem notes are played with the left hand.
The D notes in parentheses may be omitted to facilitate the lever changes.

by Felix Mendelssohn
harp arrangement by Sylvia Woods

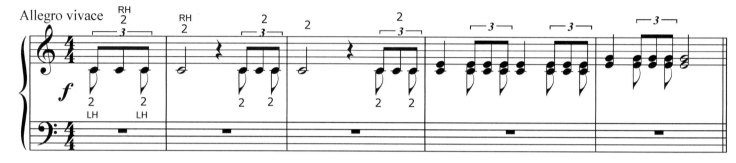

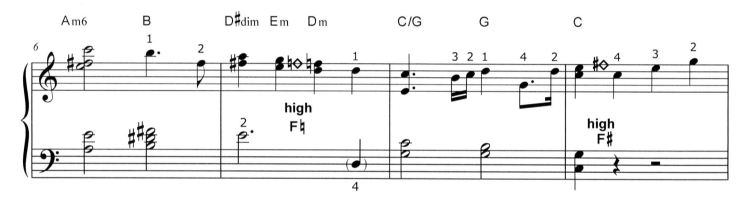

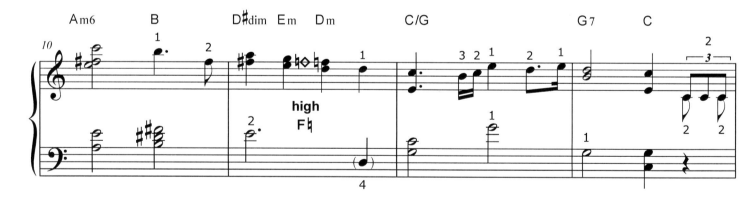

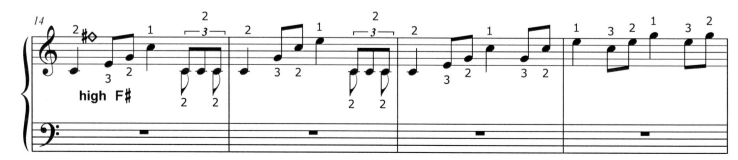